# WHAT IS YOUR MOTIVATION?

WONDRA SPENCER

*Before writing this motivational journal, I had the vision to share my motivations with the World, and I give all the glory to God!*

*I want to dedicate this journal to my beautiful grandmother Hilda, my kids Elijah and Eliana, my husband Freddie, family, and friends, and remember, anything is possible!*

# INTRODUCTION

What is your motivation? Have you ever considered why you are not accomplishing your goals? Your energy was high-spirited and ready to take over the world! In 2010, I was thinking the same way with a new premature baby boy, Elijah. I had to kick myself in the butt and make myself get serious, not for me but for my son. I considered buying diapers, paying for utilities, and the basic daily necessities. If I struggled to do those basic things, I knew it was time to revisit my current goals. As we journey through the things that keep me motivated, I hope you can take the time for yourself, get motivated, accomplish your goals, and **REMEMBER that** it is never too late!

The topics of my goals are family, debt, and health, with my favorite biblical verse at the end of the paper, which I place in my Bible yearly. I started the goal writing with a long-time friend from grade school and work. In this way, she wrote her yearly goals and shared them. I loved the idea and did the same thing. If you are not religious, write your goals and set them somewhere you know to find them—examples include placing them on the refrigerator, taping them to your mirror, or anywhere easily accessible.

## *Yearly goals*

The yearly goals shouldn't be dreadful to you! In January yearly, I write out my plans and read the previous year's goals. If needed, I will continue them and celebrate my accomplishments. For instance, once I completed my degree, I bought one of my favorites. My favorites are lovely handbags, a spa date with myself, and an enjoyable family vacation. Meanwhile, my spa date is yearly, during my birthday. It is one of my self-care dates. My favorite part of the family vacation is unlimited time and relaxing with the family.

## Family

I selected goals for my family because they might have plans for themselves, and I can continue to have unique goals for them. My goal for my family is to have them be healthy and live a relevant life. Sometimes, your family is not thinking about their goals, but you can instill goodness in them. Don't stop pursuing your goals under any circumstances!

## Savings

You want to have an emergency savings account for emergencies only. You want at least $500-$1,000 in your emergency savings banking at all times. Some examples of when to use your emergency savings include new car engines, car tires, career loss, and many more. Non-emergency items include a new pair of shoes due to attending a local concert and a new pair of jeans because they are cute, and you get the concept of the emergency and non-emergency items.

## Debt

The next goal is debt because everyone wants to be debt free. Here, the number of years when you want to be debt free, such as one, two, five, or six years from now, with the name of the goal. Do you want to be debt free? Such as clearing a mortgage, student loan, or credit card? Once you pay off the smallest to the most significant deficit, give yourself a high five because the debt is complete. Your next step is to take the debt money and place it into a savings account or an investment. For example, if your debt totaled $300, you want to take the money and open a savings or investment account.

## Health

What do you think about your health? If your health is excellent, write a goal to keep it *immaculate*. If you have some work to do with your health, work on it and write it down. If you do not complete your goals, encourage yourself, rewrite them yearly, and keep at them until they are complete. Improving your health could increase your chances of living a longer life and decrease stressors. But stress plays a vital role in your health. A suggestion for your health goal is to complete joyful exercises such as yoga, speedwalking, or things to improve your overall health.

## Dream

It is never too late to stop dreaming. But have you thought about making your dreams a reality? If you make your dreams a reality, you feel great about yourself and your accomplishments. We only live once and make the most of it! Because it is **NEVER** too late to make dreams come true. My grandmother Hilda said, Wondra, take one class a semester and achieve your career goals. I didn't listen initially, but before she passed away in 2014, I earned my Associate's degree in Health Information Management and obtained my Registered Health Information Management certification. I was so happy I had achieved my goal, and she knew it! Along the way, I had haters on my team that I removed from my circle and stuck to my plans. You can do the same!

## Positivity

Do you surround yourself with positivity? I asked myself the same thing. If your circle is not favorable, re-think the individuals of your process and re-create it. Is the issue you? I took the time to date myself and love myself before I could love anyone. I am a work-in-process. To me, achieving the little tasks is enormous, and I will pat myself on the back for achieving them.

If you don't love yourself, then who will love you? I went to the movies, lunches, and dinner with myself and loved it. Take time and get to know yourself and surround yourself with positive individuals. It is okay to have a bad day, but turn it into a joyous one. My joyful day is opening the window with wind and sunshine on my skin, brisk walking, listening or dancing to my favorite artist, and spending time with family and friends.

## Conclusion

I am still on the journey to achieve my goals, always making dreams a reality and positively surrounding myself with great individuals. Once you start achieving goals, it is hard to stop because you feel so great about them and yourself.

I hope you feel motivated by sharing the techniques I learned over the years. My tasks for you are to write out your goals, make your dreams a reality, create a positive environment, and continue to inspire yourself daily. I will ask you again what your motivation is.

# GOALS

# DREAMS

# EMERGENCY SAVINGS

# DECREASE DEBT

# INFLUENCES

# FAVORITE SONGS/ARTISTS

# SELF-CARE DAY

# HEALTH

# RE-ACCESS YOUR THOUGHTS FROM A NEGATIVE TO A POSITIVE